Why Are They Like That? Young and Old

Questions you've dared to ask, answered by real people, celebrities and experts

A book series based on the award-winning sharing project that's captured worldwide attention helping people in their personal, social and business relationships

Phillip J. Milano

For Robin, Jacob, Lucas and Ben

Publisher:
Y Forum
yforum@yforum.com

ISBN: 978-1-07-983836-7

Cover and interior layout by Sandy Weber,
Key 3 Creative, Jacksonville, Florida
Cover photo credit: Rawpixel. Stock photo for illustrative purposes
only; any person depicted is a posed model.

Content based in part on the popular Y? sharing project and Dare
to Ask column

Find out more about the author, upcoming books and speeches at
www.phillipmilano.com, www.facebook.com/PhillipJMilano or
@PhillipMilano.

Books In This Series

Why Are They Like That? Blacks

Why Are They Like That? Whites

Why Are They Like That? Hispanics

Why Are They Like That? Asians

Why Are They Like That? Gay Men

Why Are They Like That? Lesbians

Why Are They Like That? Women

Why Are They Like That? Men

Why Are They Like That? Rich and Poor

Why Are They Like That? Religious (or not)

Why Are They Like That? Disabled People

Why Are They Like That? Young and Old

Praise for the Y? sharing project and the book "I Can't Believe You Asked That!" (Perigee)

"Milano is quietly revolutionizing cross-cultural communication..."
- Pulitzer Prize-winning columnist Leonard Pitts

"If you've ever hesitated to ask a question because you think it might be considered insensitive or impolitic, now is your chance ... Nothing is considered out of bounds..."
- CNN Headline News

"(It) tells more about who we are and how we feel about each other than you're likely to learn from a dozen sociology texts…"
- Washington Post News Service

"Mr. Milano has dared to open the field of debate to the maximum…"
- Le Monde, Paris

"(A) remarkable contribution to cross-cultural understanding…"
- The (London) Guardian

"A truly rare achievement … has the potential to have a profound impact on the way we all see and understand each other..."
- Playboy magazine

"It's an incredible book. It diffuses everything ... Nothing is off limits, and the questions have that childlike honesty to them..."
- Dee Snider, Twisted Sister; host, "Dee Snider Radio"

"A take-no-prisoners attitude prevails between the volume's covers . . . This book is hard to put down..."
- Midwest Book Review

"A+ (highest rating) … Everything you wanted to know but were afraid to ask gets tackled here ..."
- Entertainment Weekly

CONTENTS

Introduction

Why Are They Like That? is a series of books based on an award-winning worldwide sharing project in which real people, experts and celebrities talk about things that make us different from each other. Silly things. Sad things. Funny things. Profound things.

Read with an open mind and we believe that by the time you're finished you'll have a much better understanding of how to make more and real friends, money and love. It's that simple.

Why? Because this isn't about trying to get ahead with diversity training. We are well beyond that. According to the Census Bureau, by 2050 the United States will have no racial or ethnic minority.

No, this is about moving past talking about how to understand each other to talking to each other. Right now.

That's why there's no agenda to these books other than getting the conversation going. We can discuss studies and methods for elevating social consciousness all we want, but there is no substitute for real dialogue.

That's where Why Are They Like That? stands apart from other books on the topic. You will see how people talk about their real differences of race, religion, sex, disability and more.

The success of the approach is proven: It's based on the ground-breaking Y? website project, blog and column that have attracted millions of visitors and worldwide media attention.

Our hope is that by reading, you will become more comfortable asking and answering the questions yourself, expecting the unexpected in return and helping change the ground rules for how we learn from and about each other. To that end, we wrap up each book in the series with our O.U.T.L.O.U.D. Method for Dialogue, with tips to help you get your own conversations started. Ultimately, that is what this effort is all about.

After all, if you want to make more friends, money and love, you better know the people you're talking to, selling to or opening to. Knowledge isn't just power. It's all power.

Enjoy.

Phillip J. Milano
Founder, Y?

'Their' music isn't for kids' ears?

They asked:

What do people think of teens listening to classic rock? My friends and I like Led Zeppelin, and, for the most part, older adults comment positively. However, we have encountered a few who've given us grief for liking "their" music.

Emily, 16, Toronto

You said:

Many of my peers don't understand why I enjoy the music my parents enjoy. And a few adults think I'm attempting to give the impression of maturity. The majority of adults, however, have no qualms about my tastes. I feel having a common link with other generations provides an excellent way to maintain communication.

J., 14, female, Jacksonville

Some old gas-bag telling you not to listen to "their" music is like a Slovak telling you not to like holupki or an Englishman telling you not to like tea.

Tony, 51, Binghamton, N.Y.

I was in Burger King once wearing a Beatles T-shirt. The guy behind the counter, in his mid-40s, looks at me condescendingly and says, "Aren't you a little young to be listening to The Beatles?" I just laughed it off and thought, "Aren't you a little old to be working behind the counter at Burger King?"

Kristen, 22, Buffalo, N.Y.

We found:

We'll let two classic rock lead guitarists do the talking to ease Emily's concern about the uptight adults in her life.

First, Little Steven Van Zandt, he of Bruce Springsteen and the E Street Band and "The Sopranos," and host of "Little Steven's Underground Garage" (undergroundgarage.com), which promotes old and new rock 'n' roll and airs on radio stations across the country and SiriusXM.

"No. 1, it's hard to believe someone would even say that. She's hanging around with the wrong adults," he said. "No. 2, the '50s and '60s and a brief part of the '70s were basically our Renaissance Period and had the greatest music ever made. It will resonate throughout our culture and inform our culture for decades and perhaps longer, until new instruments are invented.

"She should tell those people they should be listening to new garage rock and not be so close-minded. Rock 'n' roll transcends age groups, generations and time. Rock 'n' roll is forever, and cool is forever, and it has nothing to do with how old you are or what era you came out of."

Next, Rick Nielsen of Cheap Trick (cheaptrick.com):

"Kids today, just 'cause they're supposed to like rap and hip-hop or heavy metal or goth, well, if you don't like it, you don't have to go with what people think," he said. "There's great hip-hop, great rap and great old stuff, and there's crap hip-hop, crap rap and crap old stuff.

"Adults who say that to a kid must feel threatened. If someone likes something, keep your mouth shut and let the music do the talking. Don't try to force-feed anybody. That would make me want to listen more, anyway. It's just reverse psychology. So, yeah: Parents, tell your kids to quit listening to Cheap Trick! Maybe they'll start to listen to us."

15 years apart, but he wants to ask her out

They asked:

What do others think about dating older women? I am intimidated about asking a particular woman out because I'm 23 and she's 38. Any suggestions?

Dustin, Houston

You said:

It's a great idea. We're always hearing about how older men score young babes, so prove it works the other way, too.

Jeff, 45, Victoria, British Columbia, Canada

Most women I know, myself included, hate the show-off kind. If you've known this woman a while and know her likes and dislikes, ask her to join you in an activity you both enjoy. A film festival or art gallery tour. Close to the end of the tour, film or whatever, ask her to join you for coffee or dinner. Don't push. If she is not interested, she will let you know.

Reesa, 37, Ellensburg, Wash.

Sorry Dustin, but unless a 38-year-old woman was looking for some hot sex with a young stud like you, she would not want to date you. I suspect you're interested in her for sex as well. What could you two possibly have in common other than sexual attraction? [But] take a chance. Just don't be hurt when she "hits it and quits it." Women are just as good at doing that as men are.

Rhonda O., 43, Laurelton, N.Y.

We found:

Ivana Trump (ivanatrump.com), ex of The Donald, is known for holding younger men in high esteem. And in her Oxygen network reality special "Ivana Young Man," she counseled a well-to-do older woman pursued by eight 20-something studs. We'll assume she's an expert in this area.

Ivana tells us young Dustin should — no, must — go there.

"If you like this woman, then ask her out," she said by e-mail. "She can only say yes, no, or even maybe. ... If she's terrific, and open, and happy with her life, she'll probably say yes and you both get a great evening out. ... Younger men/older women or vice-versa are nothing new or controversial anymore. The most important fact of life is that we live it, fully, daily and with no regrets. You've got a long road ahead of you, so get rid of the fear and trepidation, and as Nike tells us, just do it!"

Doing it they are. AARP The Magazine found that of 1,407 men and 2,094 women aged 40 to 69 it surveyed, a third of the women who date are going out with younger men.

"Older women are dating younger men because there are fewer men at their age level at this time in their lives," said AARP Senior Research Advisor Xenia Montenegro, who helped prepare the report. "You have to expand your market."

It doesn't hurt that older women are taking better care of themselves, and that changing sexual mores mean Baby Boomer lasses can now hook up easier with Gen-X or Y lads — see "Cougar Town" and other shows for reference.

But it's not all about sex for older women. "They wouldn't mind having it, but they have more of a need for companionship, for someone who respects them," Montenegro said.

'That is a horrible thing to do to someone'

They asked:

Is there a nudist camp in Europe that can handle my request that my son of 14 be made to stay completely nude for an entire stay next summer when he is out of school?

Megan, 34, nudist, Paris

You said:

That is a horrible thing to do to someone.

Norbert, 17, Minnesota.

If my parent forced me to be nude, whether I liked it or not, I would hate them and question their motives. Camp is supposed to be fun, not a summer of hell.

Britt, female, Washington, D.C.

That's called "child abuse." I'm not sure what you think you're accomplishing by planning to shove your lifestyle down his throat, but ... he'll hate you for the rest of his life. Have fun with that.

Ann, 39, Kansas City, Mo.

Don't most parents "shove" their lifestyle down their kids' throats?

Rochelle, Williston, N.D.

We found:

We're not sure what they make young'uns do in those high-falutin' Europe parts, but in these good ol' U.S. of A. parts, we don't like to force 'em to show their parts.

Sure, we may dress our 5-year-olds in stripper-tops that say "Juicy" or "You Want This" on them, but just because someone's got a sleazy mom, does anyone really put stock in that famous saying about the apple not falling far from the stripper pole?

Nicky Hoffman Lee of the 25,000-member Naturist Society (naturistsociety.com), which "promotes body acceptance through clothing-optional recreation," said most 14-year-olds are body-conscious and don't want to be naked.

"And they're certainly not going to a camp with Mom and Dad. That's all teens, not just naturists."

The worst thing to do is force them, she said.

"They might be very embarrassed. And I'm sorry to say, but if a child is very upset and talks about it and it gets out, a mother could lose custody."

But are there long-term negative psychological effects on a kid going natural?

"I don't think so. We've done polls and found that just about everyone has skinny-dipped with others at some point. The key thing is it has to be their choice."

Some might wonder if it's OK at all to raise a child in a nudist culture. Hoffman said that first, measures are taken to protect children at resorts or beaches, through self-policing and guidelines. More importantly, letting it all hang out fosters a healthy body image.

"We call our parts by the appropriate names and aren't ashamed of them. There's no 'pee-pee' in naturism. We know our parts and what they are for."

Naturists tend to have lower numbers of teen pregnancies, she said. Girls and boys learn about inappropriate actions, and how not to clamor for attention or denigrate themselves or others "imperfections."

"They end up with a deeper respect for the opposite sex," she said. "It's like there's no surprises. We look deeper than the surface ... you may grow up feeling intimidated talking to a doctor if he's got his suit and tie on, but when there's no clothes on anyone, it's an even playing field."

13

Are teens going at it more than in the past?

They asked:

Why do most adults assume I'm sexually active because I'm a teen?
J.B., 15, male, Bloomfield Hills, Mich.

You said:

For the most part, teens are. Another factor might be your looks. If you're attractive, most people will assume you're sexually active.
Craig, 21, Canada

Because for many of today's teens, that's the stereotype. Hang in there. It's tough, but you'll get through.
Sophisticated lady, 22, Jacksonville

We found:

Teens really are doing it less, and being safer about it. According to a Kaiser Family Foundation study, a little less than half of all high school students say they've gone all the way these days, down from 54 percent in 1991. And 62 percent used a condom, compared to only 57 percent in 1997.

So what makes people think it's a Teens Gone Wild world? The media are one culprit, says University of Florida journalism professor Kim B. Walsh-Childers. She studies media effects on adolescent sexual attitudes and behavior, and co-edited the book "Sexual Teens, Sexual Media."

"It breeds an image ... that not only are they out there attacking all things that walk, but that they are totally emotionless about it. I think that's not entirely true."

Research is clear that TV influences teen attitudes about sex. Studies show that three-quarters of teens say sex on TV influences the sexual behavior of kids their age. Meanwhile, a Rand Corp.

14

survey found that teens who viewed lots of sexual content were twice as likely to initiate sexual intercourse.

And sexual content there is: Another Kaiser study found that 70 percent of all shows contain sexual talk or behavior. With so much of it out there, teens and adults alike may have a skewed notion of just how much sex is going on in real life, Walsh-Childers said.

"People who watch a lot of TV will tend to overestimate, for example, the percentage of people who have extramarital affairs," she said. "The joke is not that married people don't have sex, but that they just don't have it with each other."

Of course, it doesn't help adults' views when today's teens appear to be more narcissistic, baring their souls and more online and via texting (and sexting). But some of that may get more media attention than it deserves, further skewing things, Walsh-Childers added.

Besides, "if kids have started acting sexy, all we have to do is look at advertising," she said. "We start telling them when they are prepubescent that it's a good thing to look sexy ... like selling thong underwear for 10-year-old girls."

But don't expect things to get toned down in the TV ratings game.

"Let's be honest, the grand struggles over downloading songs to an iPod or which phone you might get, there's not as much interest in."

Preps, skaters, jocks, geeks ... who are they?

They asked:

What's the definition of a sk8ter (skater) and a prep?

Michelle, 14, Battle Creek, Mich.

You said:

I've always heard that a skater was the same as a slacker: One who does not try too hard.

Bill L., 40, Vermont

A skater skateboards a lot. "Prep" is for someone who's clean-cut, fairly popular, does well in school and maybe wears khaki regularly.

S.R., 21, female, Austin

When "skater" is mentioned, most people will probably immediately think of a long-haired, dirty, tight-jean-wearing pothead. The other common skater look would be a New Era baseball hat with a big shirt and semi-baggy jeans. No matter what they're wearing, "pothead" is always included. But most people who fit the description of "pothead, burnout," etc., don't skateboard. It's hard to nail down a clear description of an actual skater, just like it would be for a hockey player or a painter.

H., 18, male, Clay County, Fla.

We found:

"Skaters"? "Preps"? What are those? Don't we demean Skaterpreps when we try to break them down into meaningless, obscure subcategories? Many fine, stoned Skaterpreps are just trying to get by in their Acuras® with battered kicker ramps sticking out of the trunk, wearing Aeropostale® shirts while fleeing public sidewalk rent-a-cops, and texting their friends on their iPhone® to see if that "footy" of their kick-flip backsmith got uploaded to Vimeo yet.

Not to mention all the Emojocks, Nerdgoths and Gangstercheerleaders who blanch at being subdivided.

But Murray Milner Jr. did, amazingly, analyze these subgroups, for his book "Freaks, Geeks, and Cool Kids: American Teenagers, Schools, and the Culture of Consumption." A professor emeritus of sociology at the University of Virginia, he spent parts of three years observing youths in high schools and getting more than 250 accounts describing peer structures from students in 27 states.

He found that high schools have become more pluralistic, but traditional hierarchies still exist at "a fair number" of them, with jocks and preps at the top, skaters toward the lower end, and nerds, well, still feeding off the bottom.

With a disclaimer that his research is now several years old, Milner offered that preps tended to be perceived as more popular, upper-middle class, dressing more traditionally, usually identified more with alcohol and feeling social pressure, and concerned with grades, if not intellectual matters. Skaters were seen as overwhelmingly male, more alienated from their peers, totally focused on skateboarding and associated with drug use.

"Initial observations about these differences come from teens themselves, and then movies and media images crystallize and exaggerate these distinctions for dramatic purposes," he said. "Those images get fed back, and it affects students' sense of what it means to be such and such.

"And then the feedback loop goes on ..."

Does (car) size matter as you age?

They asked:

Why do so many elderly people drive Crown Victorias or huge Buicks?

Chris, 34, female, Madisonville, Ky.

You said:

I think you have to be 100 in order to buy a Buick Century.

Andrew, Salt Lake City

My guess is it's a combo of comfort (big-boat cars are easier on old-people joints) and the Depression-era desire to "buy American."

K., 28, female, *Minneapolis*

My grandpa does the same thing! For him it was the last company car he had (back in 1979) and reminds him of his friend who passed away back about that time.

Vanessa, 19, Fargo, N.D.

As a member of a senior family, I can tell you our reasons for wanting a larger vehicle: space-space-space, and comfort. When you are traveling on the interstates at 60 to 70 mph, you have a lot more confidence in a larger vehicle.

Senior citizen, Port St. Joe

Old people only appear to drive large cars. There are several phenomena at work: First, old people drive very slowly and, as hypothesized by Einstein and proved by Doppler in his seminal work Aunt Tillie's Studebaker and the Reverse Doppler Effect, slow-moving objects appear longer than fast-moving objects. For example, orbiting Space Shuttle astronauts reported difficulty distinguishing between the Great Wall of China and John Glenn's wife driving her Honda Civic. In addition, old people shrink, making the car look larger.

B. Hale, 43, male, Hartford, Conn.

We found:

Well done, B. Hale. Well done. Now hand back the mic and find your seat, please. Drinks on us.

Buicks and Crown Victorias indeed remain favorite rides of the older set

According to J.D. Power and Associates, the average age of all car buyers is around 47. But Buick buyers? Average age 63. Crown Vic buyers? Average age 62.

Researchers at the Center for Urban Transportation Research at the University of South Florida wanted to see if big cars really were big with the elderly. Their study concluded that seniors do prefer cars with a longer wheelbase — the distance from front to back axle.

Veteran auto writer Brock Yates, who scribed for Car and Driver magazine for more than four decades, has no doubt why.

"It plays back into youthful memories. Plus they feel safer with that giant bulk of steel around them. . . . And old people don't have to bend down to get in."

Will the environment and fuel prices change things?

"Maybe," said Yates, who was the mastermind behind the Cannonball Baker Sea-To-Shining-Sea Memorial Trophy Dash (you may know it by its shorter name: "The Cannonball Run"). "But while all the greenies whine and [complain] about things, nobody has come up with an alternative. Nobody's really altering their living styles.

"Still, the industry is moving away from big hulks toward fuel efficiency. Those big boys are eventually going to go away."

Can a kid live without gaming, texting or tweeting?

They asked:

Many kids my age feel it is impossible to live a comfortable or happy life without a TV set and probably not without a computer. Why?

Alex, 16, male, Elkins Park, Penn.

You said:

I love my computer, but I'd live very happily without it.

Bairn, 15, female, New Zealand

We found:

We took this matter to former pro gamer Chris Lemley, an electronic sports consultant and former president of the iconic (now defunct) Team Pandemic hardcore gaming team.

So, why did you have a rotten childhood?

My parents strongly supported my hobbies. I don't think I could have had it much better. I played every sport imaginable. It's that competitive drive that often leads players into "pro gaming" in the first place; you'll find that almost all of us were athletes in some form throughout our youth.

Can you walk when you're so morbidly obese?

Let's skip the walk and grab a cart instead. I'd be more than happy to take your money on the golf course.

How do you handle your Vitamin D Deficiency Syndrome?

Why go outside when you can get a perfectly good monitor tan? Going outside would lead to seeing the world, and that's something we just don't do. (Note: Team Pandemic competed in almost a dozen countries and won championships on three continents.)

Is it bad being a loner with no girlfriend?

Oh man, one of our girl gamers has it rough. She did "Guitar Hero" promos and was on stage with Gene Simmons (Kiss), Slash (Guns N' Roses) and even the ultimate rock star, Bill Gates himself. She gets hundreds of friend requests a week, and you know they're all from gamer guys.

How often do you cry or stomp your headset when your character dies?

I better not see anyone stomp on a headset. Our sponsors wouldn't want us treating their product that way. (Team Pandemic partnered with a number of Fortune 500 companies to promote their products and services.)

Do you shave and bathe weekly, or monthly?

I'd say our gamers tend to do it monthly, or at least when it's time to go to the bank. They have to cash the checks from all their winnings.

When did you realize you were so violent?

I found online gaming at age 9 — you know, when I was "living on the streets." Seriously though, I fell in love immediately.

Adult diapers, or bedpan?

Depends.

Real or animated porn?

C'mon, have you ever seen Lara Croft? Even Angelina Jolie couldn't do her justice in the movie.

You're really a 13-year-old Korean boy, aren't you?

If I was, I'd be playing Starcraft and making serious dough.

Is letting your kid hoist a few OK?

They asked:

What is the youngest age to give alcohol to your children? Is it OK if they get drunk?

Baby Boomer, 45, male, Los Angeles

You said:

I can't think of a single reason why letting your kids drink is a good idea.

Dick, 42, Chicago

I offer my daughter a sip of whatever adult beverage she cares to try. She hates most. At some point we'll let her drink until she feels "tipsy" and then "drunk," carefully monitoring it. I want her to understand how much alcohol it takes to get to both points, so she doesn't wind up at some party at 16 or 17 dead from alcohol poisoning.

Tim, 37, Chesterfield, Mich.

I find it hard to believe a baby boomer is asking if it's OK to contribute to the delinquency of a minor.

Katie, 38, Los Angeles

The first time I got really buzzed was at a family reunion; I was about 13. I went away to college much better able to handle my alcohol, know my limits, etc. . . . I think the European model is much better than the American one in this regard.

Dave, 35, New Orleans

I wouldn't give alcohol to your children until you're at least 46.

Rich, 23, Michigan

Between the ages of 5 and 12, my grandmother used to give us kids a hot toddy made from moonshine when we were sick. Talk about toasted! But when I woke up the next morning, I had nary a sniffle.

Monika, 26, Houston

People who say never let them before 21 are giving rebellious teens a reason to drink.

Jami, 19, Pullman, Wash.

Let them get drunk? That's a form of child abuse.

Christine, 27, Minneapolis

We found:

Isn't this a moot point? These 1-year-olds are already poop-faced to begin with, wobbling all over the place, barely able to stammer out "ba-ba" for "bottle." It's epidemic.

But, for kicks, we talked to David Rosenbloom, director of the Youth Alcohol Prevention Center at Boston University's School of Public Health.

Some studies suggest — but not strongly — that "in some families, where there's a lot of family time and drinking wine with dinner is seen as a special occasion . . . the kids may be less likely to engage in early problematic drinking," he said.

But, we're talking about context and culture: having a "taste" of wine, in a setting where the practice may have been done for generations.

"Parents who provide beer or spirits under what they believe are controlled circumstances are kidding themselves that they are teaching responsible drinking," he said. "I've seen multiple cases in which parents think they can control a situation by inviting the kids in and taking the car keys away, and then having horror stories."

"This business about 'training' people to drink is horseshit. They are teaching them it's perfectly fine to drink without respect to the law or their ability to absorb it."

Listening to grandpa's golf stories -- again

They asked:

Why do old people like to talk about their golf game so much?

Ben, 9, Clay County, Florida

You said:

Old people, like young people, middle-aged people and all the people in between, like to talk about things they find interesting. I know lots of old people — my grandkids think I am an old person — and none of us golf, so none of us ever discusses it. It seems to me that you happen to know a lot of old people who are avid golfers, that's all.

Robin W., 55, Westland, Mich.

Seniors are not talking about golf, they're really talking about conversations on the golf course and off the course. So while some seniors may speak about their "handicap," they are really striking up a conversation with someone they hope is on their same level. That same chat that starts out with golf will often end up with their grandkids.

Steve C., Massachusetts

We found:

A back-nine's worth of possible answers for this wee lad:

— They're remembering stuff. You know that thought you had about nine seconds ago that you won't think about again until you're in your 50s because you've moved on to thinking about uploading your 14th YouTube video of your dog barking something that sounds like "I'm sorry"? Well, older people re-think about their recent and long-ago thoughts more frequently than that. It actually helps them. Tons of studies prove it. Gerontologists like the late Robert Butler have shown that reminiscing leads to less sadness, improved family and social relations, less chronic pain and better cognition (are you following this, sonny?).

— They aren't tweeting or texting. A Pew Research Center survey found that only one in six people older than 75 even use the Internet daily. Only 11 percent of folks older than 65 bother to text. Oddly, they're conversing instead.

— Gotta justify. Golfers spend hazardous amounts of money and time on their games. So there could be a need for talk-therapy to bring closure. National Golf Foundation stats show golfers spend more than $17 billion a year on equipment and rounds, play an average of about 60 times per year and spend $311 each on golf clothes annually.

— Ego. People like to talk about themselves and their accomplishments. Especially when they're overestimating their drives by at least 30 yards, which is what a report by golf think-tank Frankly Consulting determined.

— Running of the mouth. This may be a function of lack of sobriety. Researchers Conor P. O'Brien and Frank Lyons of Ireland found that of all sports, golf ranked fifth behind only cricket, Gaelic football, rugby and hurling (naturally) in percentage of drinkers, as well as in the percent of competitors who drank before playing.

— Your generation is "X-treme," not ours. "Emily Post and other manners experts have trained us that extreme is vulgar; moderate is good," said golf comedian T.P. Mulrooney (golfcomic.com). "That's why we've chosen a sport which allows us to eat hot dogs, swig beer and make business calls while we play."

Let me tell ya 'bout the birds and the bees and the teens

They asked:

Why don't teens cherish their virginity anymore?

Anna, 17, Memphis, Tenn.

You said:

It bothers me when friends say they went to a party and "did it" with this or that person. I'm waiting until marriage — and maybe then some. If you think about it, it has to do with a person's family background as well.

S., 15, female, Jacksonville

A lot of teenagers tend to be pressured into doing things, and from there on it's no big deal. I plan on saving it until my wedding day.

Jen, 17, Jacksonville

While my husband and I were each other's first, we did not wait until marriage. Our wedding night was hectic enough without added expectations.

Meg, 21, Gainesville

At 18, I decided I was ready to lose my virginity. No one told me the babies that would one day pass through my womb deserved it to be a place of honor.

Tami G., 34, Dallas

We found:

We could serve up some numbers that discuss what teens tell survey-takers when asked for their innermost feelings about having sex. Or we could just go ahead and tell you how many of them are doing it and get on with reality.

A Kaiser Family Foundation report found that the percentage of high school students who have sexual intercourse is down to 47 percent, a drop from 54 percent in past years.

The study also found:

— Black high school students are more likely to have gone all the way (60 percent) compared to white (44 percent) and Hispanic students (49 percent). More black high school students (14 percent) and Latino students (7 percent) initiate sex before age 13 compared to white students (4 percent).

— 26 percent of female teens and 29 percent of male teens have more than one sexual partner in their lives.

— Almost one-quarter of sexually active high school students report using alcohol or drugs during their most recent sexual encounter.

— 13 percent of those age 14-24 report they have sexted a naked photo or video of themselves.

However, Jonathan Klein, former chairman of an American Academy of Pediatrics (aap.org) committee on teen pregnancy, said he hasn't noticed a big change in how teens value virginity. A more relevant question, he said, is whether they can discuss decisions they make about their sexual behavior openly with their parents and health care providers.

"The right place to talk about values is with parents who aren't judgmental about what [health care] services might be offered," he said. "If you frame it as being about virginity, you miss the point that all our teens need to make decisions about how to be responsible. ... We recommend giving them comprehensive health reproductive information."

And before parents get too complacent because of the lower numbers: "technical virginity" — not having sex but engaging in other sexual behaviors such as oral — is rising among teens, according to data from the Centers for Disease Control.

"So it's important for parents to talk with their teens about their expectations and values," Klein said. "Those kinds of discussions can have a big impact on how teens choose to act."

He's 10 and still sleeps with mom – is that ... OK?

They asked:

My ex-wife continues to sleep with our 10-year-old son when he stays at her house. This is not a sexual thing. Is this unusual?

Joe, 51, Florida

You said:

I would be worried. Ten-year-old boys are coming into their sexual maturity soon, and they don't need to wake up with their mom lying next to them.

Sheri, 41, San Francisco

Your ex-wife is forming a closer bond. The mother has the power to impact her child for life. Your ex-wife feels it's not wrong to sleep with her 10-year-old son as long as the tie produces a healthy relationship. I concur.

L.C., Greenville, Miss.

She's way over-attached, and it might not be overtly sexual, but there's a serious "ick" factor, which will only get ickier as your son gets closer to puberty.

A., female, Missouri

If you're sure it's not in a sexual way, and the child is developing in a "normal" manner (he's not acting out sexually, he's developing appropriate boundaries, etc.), and she's not exposing him to her sexual activity, I'd say you're overreacting. There are cultures where the communal bed is kept for the entire life of a child.

Shelly, 49, New Alexandria, Pa.

We found:

As with most issues, there are two sides to this mattress. Developmental psychologist Aletha Solter, founder of The Aware

Parenting Institute (awareparenting.com) and author of "Helping Young Children Flourish," tucks in on the softer side, so to speak.

"It is normal for children to want closeness and reassurance at night whenever there is stress in their lives, because stress increases a child's attachment needs. Divorce of the parents can be a very stressful experience for children," she said by e-mail.

"Many children feel that their family has fallen apart, and they often blame themselves or fear that their parents will stop loving them. If [the] son is unable to sleep alone because of chronic anxiety, it might be a good idea for him to see a competent psychotherapist."

Not to throw rocks in that bed, but Kevin Kennedy, senior child psychologist with Harvard Vanguard Medical Associates (harvardvanguard.org) in Boston, says, uh-uh.

Occasional visits to the parents' bed at scary times are OK, but overall (in U.S. culture at least): "It's not a good idea in terms of promoting autonomy. Kids should gain independence and ability to do things by themselves, like sleeping."

In divorces, where the child may seek increased closeness, Kennedy suggests running errands or completing projects together more often.

"Sometimes divorced parents respond in terms of their own need of companionship. It's [sleeping together] done under the guise of sensitivity to the child, but the parents are really meeting their own needs."

And as a child gets older, things can get trickier.

"It's treacherous territory when kids are 10 or 11, in pre-adolescence, where erotic aspects can be a factor," he said. "I advise parents to never do it."

29

Like, um, are you going out with him, or what?

They asked:

Why are younger teenagers so obsessed with "who likes whom" and going out with people, and call sensible people who don't care about anything like that gay or geeky?

Brandon, 13, Jacksonville

You said:

Once hormones kick in, all you want to do is make out with people. Then it comes down to reputation: Even if the person is a total moron, if he's a great kisser, you've got to date him.

Claire, 15, Fernandina Beach

Teenagers in America go from being treated like little kids straight to being "grown-ups," so dating is a way for them to feel more grown up. Or, it could be there isn't anything on TV, and they're bored.

Stephanie S., Washington, D.C.

Kids your age are . . . trying to work out their status in the pack, and trying to get a handle on urges and feelings none of you really had as recently as a year or two prior. Labeling outsiders is a defense mechanism.

Ann, 40, Missouri

It all has to do with the beliefs subtly taught by American society: 1) In order to be happy, you have to have a partner; 2) You're not "complete" until you've found your "better half;" and 3) If you wait too long, you may never find them and die a lonely old man or woman.

Shelly, Pennsylvania

You're in for a lot worse in your latter teens, so enjoy this relatively innocuous "who likes whom" stuff while you still can.

Craig, 21, Duncan, Canada

We found:

Of course teens are the only ones obsessed with who's dating whom. Adults don't give a hoot — that's why you never see Web sites, magazines, TV tabloid shows and "Celebrity Watch" items in daily newspapers constantly featuring tryst gossip about Madonna, Justin, Zac, Hayden, Milo, Halle, J-Lo, George and … even Lindsay still?

For younger teens (mainly girls), fixation on dating arises because sexual attraction is growing at the same time they're looking for love and approval, said teen expert Barbara McRae, founder of TeenFrontier.com and author of "Coach Your Teen to Success." Amid increasing social pressures juiced up on social networking sites, if Mom and Dad are being overly critical or detached, dating — and talking about dating — can fill the void.

Name-calling and bullying to "fit in" may follow if no one monitors the situation, she said.

Research shows that girls start thinking about dating earlier, McRae noted.

"They stare at boys, have crushes, daydream . . . they're looking at their self-worth through the eyes of others."

So, is it all "sensible"?

"We don't know what stage of development this boy [Brandon] is at," she said. "Everyone wakes up to the opposite sex at different times; maybe he doesn't understand all the hoopla yet, so he's making it sound like he's the sensible one. And as adults, sure, we know at 13 they don't have the interpersonal skills yet for a dating situation . . . so we take it as sensible [not to date when young]."

31

Get a piercing when you're old enough to request it?

They asked:

Why do some parents have their infant's ears pierced? Why risk the child pulling her ears or getting an infection?

T., 20, female, Macomb, Ill.

You said:

I think it is selfish to get an infant's ears pierced. That baby does not come out of the womb saying, "Mummy, a dazzling pair of earrings would go quite wonderfully with my onesie, don't you agree?"

Alaina R., 28, Cincinnati

When I was 6 months old, my mom pierced my ears because I had no hair and she was tired of people saying "Oh, he is so cute!" When taken care of properly, the piercing will not get infected.

S.S., female, Branchville, N.J.

My mother had my ears pierced when I was a baby and did the same thing with my sister. I never thought about it like that, but I think most people do it when their child is a baby to get it over with.

Cee, 20, female, Philadelphia

I asked an acquaintance this after she mentioned she pierced her baby's ears. She said she felt she should, because her ears were pierced as a baby. Also, the mother could take care of cleaning them.

Stephanie, Newark, N.J.

We found:

Before we get to why it's done, let's quote from the Association of Professional Piercers' official policy on piercing minors, from www.safepiercing.org:

"For any piercing of a minor, a parent or legal guardian must be present to sign a consent form. Proof positive, state-issued photo identification is required from the legal guardian, and a bona fide form of identification from the minor. . . . Under no circumstances is it acceptable or appropriate for a piercer to perform piercing on the nipples or genitals of an individual under 18 years of age."

Piercings for infant ears have been around in Hindu and Mesoamerican culture for a long time, as a religious rite of passage or to distinguish gender early on.

Other cultures — say your typical Caucasian North American — jumped on the bandwagon in more recent decades, said Christine Whittington, co-author of "Body Marks: Tattooing, Piercing and Scarification."

"It's become more popular, like any fad," said Whittington, who has a number of piercings. "Earrings have been around for millennia. It's more natural to see the body as a canvas."

Whittington herself is cautious about infant piercings.

"I wouldn't do it; I'd want my child to have a choice. . . . You should get a piercing when you're old enough to request it without being asked, and are old enough to observe the hygiene that's needed with it."

But, different pokes for different folks.

"Some parents . . . pierce the ears when young, so the infant won't remember the pain," Whittington said.

'A danger to everybody on the road, and he knows it'

They asked:

Do older people feel it's wrong for society to ask them not to drive?

S.W., 20, female, Johnson City, Tenn.

You said:

My grandmother is a decent driver, but her boyfriend is terrible. He speeds, flips the bird and goes on a tirade if he's cut off. . . . He is a danger to everybody. But he still feels it's his right to be on the road.

Craig, 21, Duncan, Canada

Many of the residents where I work recognize it's best for their own safety and others, so they gave up their car keys long ago.

Anne C., 24, Iowa City, Iowa

I think all old people should be required to retake a special license test at age 65. It should check eyesight, hearing and basic motor skills.

Nick, 17, Cromwell, Conn.

Nick: Considering you have been driving a maximum of two whole years, you probably don't have the best clues on "good" driving.

QTCali Gurl, California

I've had several near-misses with older people because they can't see over the steering wheel of their mammoth-size Caddies.

Jen R., 28, Greenfield, Pa.

We found:

Not long ago we talked with Fred Thomas, a driving instructor at the Traffic Safety Center in Gainesville, Fla, who at 67 had brandished his dreaded clipboard for more than four decades.

No one does a jig — or jitterbug — when asked to put it in park for good, he said.

"For older men, it's part of their manhood; it's a cut on that. For women, it's an independence thing in general."

Thomas said about 90 percent of older drivers he tests do "OK," though some have vision problems or are left-foot brakers who grew up driving stick-shifts. "You hear about them driving through storefronts."

According to the National Highway Traffic Safety Administration, drivers 65 and older make up 15 percent of all licensed drivers but account for only 10.4 percent of fatal crashes, compared to drivers ages 35 to 54, who have the highest rate at 33.8 percent.

If you're concerned about an older driver, though, the NHSTA says you can seek guidance from a physician, or resources such as AAA or AARP.

Another option (we're talking scorched-earth policy here; check to see if you're in the will) is to write your state's Department of Motor Vehicles and express your concerns about the driver in question.

The DMV may test the driver. But in Florida, for example, older people can rest easy: It won't include parallel parking.

" 'Blue Power' — blue-haired ladies — lobbied against that years ago and got it repealed," Thomas said.

Mom and Dad, your teen might … like … you

They asked:

I am only 14 but feel much older. I connect more with my parents and members of their generation. My classmates do not understand me. Do any other teens feel as I do?

J., female, Jacksonville

You said:

I always enjoyed speaking with adults. But being mature for your age will leave you lonely in high school. I can't wait for college! I am trapped in a high school full of cliques and immature kids.

Deecie, 16, Chantilly, Va.

No, you aren't odd. There should be others like you who'd appreciate your friendship.

Julie, 26, Jacksonville

Don't "dumb" yourself down.

Luca, 22, Lauderdale Lakes

I still feel this way. I hate it. I find older people (and me) to almost be uptight. I try to let go of worries and have fun and talk freely about matters that don't matter.

Jessica, 17, Canada

Keep your head on straight and know that your peers will catch up with you. You'll find that they often look up to you because you're so responsible (even if they hate to admit it).

Jesse, 28, Huntington, W.Va.

I wish I would have taken advantage of being a kid — enjoying school more, friends more, and letting go of all the deep thoughts. Don't try to grow up too fast because you will never get that back.

Danielle, 21, Flint, Mich.

Be yourself. It's better to be disliked for who you are than liked for something you're not.

We found:

Who better to blame for turning a happy-go-lucky kid into an insulated, aloof teen than a mom or dad?

"Some parents raise their kids to be with them all the time. . . . [They] include them in family discussions, spend lots of time with them but don't take them out for games or sports with other kids," said Julius Licata, co-founder of TeenCentral.net for KidsPeace (kidspeace.org), a 125-year-old nonprofit focused on youths' mental health.

"Parents may think they are doing their kids a favor, but they are missing out on their childhood years, on the peer relationships they should have."

When that happens, kids end up feeling alone, thinking no one understands their feelings.

"They are looking for other kids to relate to. . . . Suppose a teen has a fight with her parents. She can feel isolated, but a friend might say, 'Well, I have an earlier curfew than you!' Then she doesn't feel so depressed, as though she's the only one going through it."

The problem is that heightened awareness of terrorism, sexual abuse, abductions and more causes parents to shelter their children. There must be a balance, Licata said. He recommended that parents steer their "mature" kids into academic, creative or sports-related activities with peers with the same interests — and to let them spread their wings some.

"If you stifle their growth, they lose a certain amount of their own personhood," he said.

Stop mumbling when I talk to you son!

They asked:

Why do teenagers mumble all the time?

Renea, 45, Orange Park

You said:

Because being articulate went the way of being neatly dressed. Many teenagers think it isn't cool to speak clearly and intelligently, the same way they do not think it is cool to wear pants that fit them properly.

Johanna, 45, Stroudsburg, Penn.

Teen years are awkward, with all the pressure to "find yourself" and manage puberty. Mumbling teenagers probably have under-developed social skills. And of course many try to deal with themselves and the world by "disengaging." In that case the mumblers probably don't know or care that they're mumbling because it all doesn't matter. The "disengaged" image is cool to some of them.

Teresa, 20, Macomb, Ill.

I never mumble. If I have something to say, I say it loud and proud! Mumbling is a way to say something out loud without it being understood. It's a way of saying something you wish you could really say.

Luke, a teen, Denver

Some do it because they're unsure whether they want others to hear what they're saying, possibly out of fear that the listener's response might be negative. It also might be a sneaky way of bothering whoever's listening.

Mike, Chicago

Teens who mumble might not realize they do it. I have a tendency to do so, and I'm 24. The misconception that if you can hear it yourself, everyone can, could be a cause.

Andy, Fenton, Mich.

We found:

Turns out all this burbling by adolescents might actually be a rite of passage — a product of our natural development.

"Researchers say Mother Nature may have worked this out well," says Doris Bucher, a speech-language pathologist with Speakeasy communication consultants in Atlanta (speakeasyinc.com).

"The mumbling comes along right about the time a teen's voice becomes rather fragile. You might notice that sometimes teens with a lot of talent, who sing or talk too much, develop a peculiar voice from the strain. It can be a result of damage to the vocal chords."

In addition, psychologically, teens are trying to pull away from the adult world that controls them and identify with their peers, and swallowing one's words is a way to detach, Bucher said.

"A good test to see if there's a problem is to watch how they talk with their friends," because chances are they enunciate just fine with their peers.

Kids start pulling away as teens because they get second-guessed a lot, she added. Parents would do well to turn up the positive reinforcement.

"There's a lot of power in articulation. If you want your ideas taken seriously, you form words clearly . . . but what if you don't have final power in the situation?"

The good news, experts say: Mumbling often stops with entrance into college or the "real world," whichever comes first.

Kids dissing their parents? Like, yeah

They asked:

I always see children and teens degrading their parents or making them look or feel stupid. Is this the parents' fault, or is it just what society is coming to?

Luz, 20, female, Illinois

You said:

I'm a high school biology teacher and you would not believe how much teens disrespect everything. I've seen them throw fits because mom took their cell phone away after they ran up the bill. The appropriate saying is "Spare the rod, spoil the child."

Erica, 25, Alexandria, La.

We can't keep in line because we aren't given a line to keep in.

J., 14, female, Jacksonville

By the time I had kids, they weren't allowed to help around the house because it would traumatize them. We weren't allowed to discipline them because a neighbor might report us for child abuse. The kids ruled the roost. As a result, we grew a generation of me, me, me people. They are starting to run our country, and it shows.

Phyl, 63, female, Texas

Don't underestimate the role of hormones.

Eric, 17, Denver

The media is saturated with ads that cater to young people. Young people, seeing everything catering to them, start believing all of it, and think they're the ones in charge.

Ed, 26, Milpitas, Calif.

We found:

We sought out Bill Cosby (well, before all *that*), because his TV kids would never have mumbled at him.

For what it still might be worth: Via e-mail he told us it was a little bit everybody's fault when kids are disrespectful, but everyone can take a bow when a kid behaves, too.

"The issue of personal conduct is influenced in a negative or positive way by the child-rearing practices of the parents, the personality of the child and the influences of family members as well as the peer group," he said.

Michael H. Popkin, meanwhile, famous for his "Active Parenting" books (activeparenting.com), tilts toward parental miscues as the main culprit for children's misbehavior.

"We live in a much more casual society, so some things are tolerated now that weren't in the past, like kids joking with their parents and smarting off. They see their parents doing it, so they feel they can do it right back. The kids have to know where the line is."

When drawing that line, remain calm, he said. Don't yell. Don't insult. Tie punishment to the offense.

"The child needs to know that if they take a certain action, then certain privileges will be removed. Don't be arbitrary. They won't respect you if you don't respect them."

Do what we say because, well, we're older than you

They asked:

Why do older people think they can use their age to get what they want from a younger person?

Patrick, 15, St. Charles, Ill.

You said:

Because they can.

Pat H., 21, Forestdale, R.I.

They use their age as an advantage because they are cranky. When arthritis sets in, it gets pretty hard not to be.

Mark, 54, Destin

Older people make decisions based on what they think will be best — not just to get things out of kids. Adults have given you food, clothing and shelter all your life. The least you could do is help them out once in a while without totally complaining about it.

John, 20, Bakersfield, Calif.

It's because they know they are older and can pull stuff on kids. You know the saying goes, "Kids should obey their elders." That's a load of crap, and older people use it to get what they want.

Marisa, 15, Illinois

After years giving of ourselves, our time and our money to the younger generation as well as our elder generation, there is an expectancy that as we age, it is time for receiving. Unfortunately, the younger generation has no appreciation for the sacrifices made for them. They feel nothing is owed and nothing should be done unless something is in it for themselves. What a sad thing for us, them and their children, who will never learn the enjoyment of helping for the sake of helping.

Patricia, 63, Slidell, La.

We found:

Old people want their props, just like young people, says Huffington Post columnist Eric Kingson, a Syracuse University professor of social work who studies intergenerational issues.

"For most people who have moved through life, it's not unreasonable to expect some respect. But they can't try to control a child just by saying 'I'm older.' They might say 'I have some experience ...'?"

The good news is that there is, in fact, something in it for younger people when they defer to an elder, he said: Holding a door or giving up a seat means they're learning good manners and to respect others and themselves.

Seniors don't get a free pass. They should give back to society as long as they're able, he said.

Another expert, Nicholas Cummings, former president of the American Psychological Association and now in his 90s, emailed us that older people often feel ignored.

"We have all seen the occasional male curmudgeon, and the legendary cantankerous old lady. But most seniors hurt in silence under all situations in which they don't seem to count, and the fact is that most younger persons look right through them as if the senior is invisible . . . Time and time again I see young people sitting in [bus] seats while frail elderly are standing. There is very seldom an attempt to relinquish the seat, and I have never seen a senior complain about it."

Why? Because he said so.

OK to put on the white makeup and black clothes and go Goth?

They asked:

My mom said I could wear Gothic clothes as long I don't do devil worship. Then her mood went bad about it. And my dad is totally against it. I thought I had found something I liked. Any advice?

River, 12, male, Heath, Ohio

You said:

My boyfriend is Goth and is hard-working, hardly drinks and doesn't worship the devil. Ask your parents to let you dress how you want a few months. If your grades and attitude keep improving, you keep doing it. If they slip, you stop.

Michele, 31, New Orleans

Tell your mom to take pictures of you so when you have matured she can show you how utterly stupid you looked as a child.

Therocdoc, Aurora, Colo.

My granddaughter went Goth and found there was nothing but pressure from all around. It meant nothing but a lot of clothes she'd throw away soon anyhow. Are you the type of person who must be leered at by strangers to have people notice you?

D.L.P., Jacksonville

I'm a Jehovah's Witness but wear Goth. My dad doesn't like it. He makes me go to the Kingdom Hall. But when I am at school I am Gothic. I have worshipped the devil before, but then I pray to Jehovah about what I did. You can wear black, just not at church.

Olivia, 12, St. Louis

All Goths want to do is be depressed, pale, uninspired and stoned. Pick a scene where people actually want to do something and not just play dress-up.

Sker, Tulsa, Okla.

My daughter is heavily into the punk scene. But at 17 she has a lot of freedom, and she got there by earning my trust: good grades, no alcohol or drugs, calling when I tell her to and being home when she's agreed to be.

Randy, 46, Philadelphia

We found:

Goth began as a musical subculture during the post-Punk era of the late '70s, with bands like Bauhaus, Joy Division and Siouxsie and the Banshees. Some call the culture introspective and brooding, others reflective and laid-back, says Patrick Rodgers, a major Goth promoter and owner of Dancing Ferret Discs (dancing-ferret.com).

"Any club bouncer will tell you the nights they enjoy working most are Goth night. Goths don't get into fights. It attracts for the most part quiet, creative people who feel they are not accepted socially in the wider group."

They're not heavily into drugs or the occult, either, he added.

"Journalists don't talk to the woman in her early 30s who's a doctor and Catholic but comes to the Goth club on weekends. That's not as scandalous as the 16-year-old who says he's a Satanist."

This boy's parents are likely concerned how others will perceive them — that their neighbors will assume they failed as parents, Rodgers said.

"He has to explain why he's interested in Goth. Is he into the fashion? Does he just want to assert himself? Or is he depressed? Finding that out could open a dialogue."

Besides, Goths can become tight with each other, Rodgers noted, forming a support network that's handy when more typical adolescent woes like money or school problems arise.

Grab some Irish Spring and hit the shower, old man (please)

They asked:

Why do many senior citizens view a daily shave (for men) as virtually mandatory, while daily bathing of the whole body is pretty much a matter of personal preference? I would feel dirty if I did not shower daily. I would much rather have clean hair and a full beard, washed daily, than be meticulous about my facial hair and have the rest of my body unwashed.

Augustine, 39, male, Columbia, S.C.

You said:

I think there are two answers to why male senior citizens shave every day. First, it's become a habit after doing it almost every day while we worked. Second, we think it makes us look neater. There is probably a third reason for some (like me): My beard looks lousy. As for showering, as you get older and less active, you do not sweat much and aren't in a very dirty environment, so bathing may not be needed daily.

Raymond, 57, Portsmouth, Va.

Keeping yourself presentable, either through shaving daily or maintaining a well-groomed beard, garners respect. A stubbly face represents a middle ground between these societal standards of presentability. It may convey a sense the man is lazy.

Robin, 25, female, Pittsburgh

I wore a shirt, suit and tie for more than 40 years and showered and shaved every day. When I retired . . . I continued to shower every day but cut the shaving to every other day plus Sunday. Recently I have found myself not showering every day, especially in the winter, and going as much as four days without a shower or shave. In cold weather I can do this with no discomfort, odors or problems. No complaints from anyone — including my wife, children, friends, neighbors and dog.

Bill, 68, Lansdale, Pa.

We found:

Older men who grew up in the era of the "Saturday night bath" fell in line with modern cleanliness standards upon entering the workforce, says Scott Omelianuk, former style editor of GQ and former executive editor of Esquire magazine. And they may slip back into their youthful habits when they retire.

"As recently as the '30s and '40s, most houses had one bathroom, just that one utilitarian spot," said Omelianuk, co-author of "Things a Man Should Know About Style." "So you couldn't take a shower before school if you had three brothers and a father and mother getting ready for the day, too."

Also, let's face it, you can fool folks for a while when you don't bathe, but not if your face starts getting bristly.

"Shaving is a matter of pride, a quick and superficial way to still seem like you're keeping up appearances," he said.

Besides, Americans' captivation with hygiene didn't take root until the '50s, after many of today's older men had become adults, Omelianuk noted.

"It became an obsession, this idea of cleanliness and of body odor being a terrible thing. Before then, if you were a guy, you showered when you had a date. I suspect doctors today would say that hand- and face-washing are important, but that full body-washing is not always necessary."

The O.U.T.L.O.U.D. Method to Dialogue

OPEN UP: This is mostly about opening up to yourself. Why do you want to engage someone? Is it for the right reasons? The answers might help you figure out how to approach another person. A friend once told me the real reason I started Y? wasn't for me to learn more about "Buddhists in Asia or lesbians in San Francisco," but because I wanted to learn something more about myself. He was right. Acknowledging that has helped give me perspective when considering others' answers.

USE YOUR HEAD: Plan for the right question. Not all questions need to be the "wet dogs" variety. Stereotypes and clichés don't work as well as sincere attempts to talk.

TIME IT RIGHT: Create the "O.U.T.L.O.U.D. Moment". Pick your spots for provocative dialogue. Find a genuine opening rather than create a false one. It's often during those down times between all the "vital" discourse that we can most easily find a direct path to someone's point of view. If you spend enough time sitting in the cubicle next to someone of a different culture, chances are there'll come a time — over food, perhaps, or during a power outage — when the topic you've been dying to broach will wend its way naturally into the discussion.

LOCK IN ON THE TARGET: Keeping things simple can give the best chance for getting another's trust and a meaningful reply. Some of the best questions at Y?, those that prompt the most telling answers, are also often the easiest to digest. Remember, it's not about winning your point. It's what comes from the heart that counts most — and captures people's interest. Talking from the heart also means easing into things by letting someone know *why* it would help you to learn the answer to your question before you ask it.

OWN UP TO ASSUMPTIONS: One of the most refreshing and repetitive surprises of the Y? project is the difficulty in predicting how a person will respond to a question. Blacks do not think in lockstep. Nor do whites. Nor Christians or Muslims. Nor gays or straights. Be receptive to another's ideas. Wipe the slate clean and listen to the content of the message, not the color or culture   of   the   messenger.

UNLOAD YOUR EXPECTATIONS: Many of us are thinner-skinned than we'll admit. When we get hit with an answer or comment we hadn't anticipated, our emotions can often get caught off-balance, and our egos get bruised. The solution: Expect the unexpected. You'll never be blindsided or taken aback by information that doesn't gibe with your worldview.

DIGEST THE DIALOGUE: Learning about others doesn't stop when the talking's over. Assess what you're told and how it fits with or departs from your perspectives. Recap your discussion with a third party to distill the most relevant information into its most meaningful points.

ABOUT THE AUTHOR

Phillip J. Milano is the founder of Y? The National Forum on People's Differences, the acclaimed cross-cultural dialogue project that encourages people to ask unflinching, politically incorrect questions about our differences.

Since its creation in 1998, Phillip's web site, YForum.com, has attracted millions of visitors and thousands of questions and answers. He has been featured on CBS, CNN, BET and the BBC, and in numerous newspapers, including The Washington Post, New York Times and USA Today.

He is the author of the Perigee book "I Can't Believe You Asked That!" as well as writer of the pioneering newspaper column/blog "Dare to Ask."

Mr. Milano is a 25-year newspaper veteran. He received his Master of Business Administration from Northern Illinois University and his Bachelor of Science in Journalism from Southern Illinois University.

SPEECHES AND APPEARANCES

Mr. Milano is an in-demand speaker. For bookings, contact

Contemporary Issues Agency

809 Turnberry Drive, Waunakee, WI 53597-2256
Phone: 800-843-2179
Fax: 608-849-6311
www.CIAspeakers.com
Info@CIAspeakers.com